Shedding Light

From

My Journeys

By

DuEwa Frazier

Lit Noire Publishing
www.duewaworld.com
Copyright © 2001, 2002, 2012 DuEwa Frazier and
DuEwa M. Frazier, Lit Noire Publishing
All Rights Reserved
Printed in the USA

4th Edition

Frazier, DuEwa M.
Library of Congress Catalog Card Number: 2002091197
Shedding Light From My Journeys

I. Poetry I. African American Studies-Drama-Fiction
ISBN: 978-0-9719052-6-9

Layout, DuEwa Frazier

Shedding Light

From

My Journeys

By

DuEwa Frazier

Lit Noire Publishing

Author's Note

I am so blessed to have been given the gift to express myself through writing. God is good and is truly the light and love of my life, the source of my creative gifts and my strength. Praise and thanks! I thank my parents, Sylvia J. Wilson Frazier and Eric Frazier for giving me love, art, culture and unpredictability in my life. To my sister, Jamila Thema, much love and hugs for your support. Love to the Lash, Thornton, Hartsfield, Weaver, Wilson, Hughes, Agard and Watson families. Thank you Margaret Dismond, Dr. Joyce Jarrett, Dr. Clayton Halloway and Barbara Whitehead for supporting me in the study of literature and writing at Hampton University.

Thank you to my mentor in publishing and press building, Khalif Khalifah (Publisher, *Your Black Books Guide*) and the U.B. and U.S. Communications, Inc. family in Virginia. Thank you National Association of Black Journalists (NABJ)-St. Louis Chapter, for making me a part of your progress and supporting me to study journalism. Thanks to *The Daily Challenge*, Editor, Gareth Brown, and *MysisterMyself.com*. Thank you Angela Kinamore of *Essence* Magazine. Thank you for reinforcing cultural heritage (besides my parents), Leon Henderson and Fr. Gaiter of Cardinal Ritter College Prep and my African holistic teachers, Baba Adeyemi Oyeilumi and Sis. Mujiba Wadud for sharing your wisdom and love.

Thank you deeply, to my church family at St. Alphonsus Rock Church, Bridge Street A.W.

M.E., Rev. Cheryl Auguste and Emmanuel Baptist
Church who have given me love and inspiration.

Thank you to supporters of word arts such
as: The Brooklyn Moon Cafe, Nuyorican Poet's
Cafe, Nathan P.,host "The Nuyo,"
Wordspace, Wordstock, Nkiru Center, Dr. Brenda
Greene of Medgar Evers College, U. Penn's Kelly
Writer's House, Sista's Place, Brownstone Books,
Bar 13 and Kalamu Ya Salaam. I thank sacred
women writers and teachers: Iyanla Vanzant,
Susan Taylor, Pearl Cleage and Queen Afua for
healing words. Gracious thanks to the legendary art
of: Sonia Sanchez, Nikki Giovanni, Gwendolyn
Brooks, Ntozake Shange, Zora Neale Hurston,
Langston Hughes, Maya Angelou, James Baldwin,
Louis Reyes Rivera, The Last Poets-Abiodun
Oyewole, Amiri and Amina Baraka.

Peace and blessings to my contemporaries in
the poetic tradition who keep the breath and fire
going: The words in this book are for my
my childhood friends from the University City
"Loop" and my high school friends at Ritter and
"The U." The words in this book are for my college
friends at Hampton U. It was a "different world"
when we thought we were "taking a vacation,"
studying, dreaming and cutting up in Kennedy Hall,
McGrew Towers and #8 Woodland Rd. The words
in this book are for my star gazing, beautiful,
grown, smart and stylish sister, Jamila Thema - an
artist full of many colors. I love you with all my
heart little sis'.
And these words are for my surrogate
parents, in my life: Trudi Rodriguez (love you,
wherever you are now), Sis. Jamilah El-

5

Amin, Peju Babalola, Margaret Dismond, Robert
and Aisha Taylor-Watson, Ms. Maxine and Rev.
Cheryl Auguste. The words in this book are for the
smooth talking, basketball playing, clean dressing,
cadillac driving, folks I hung out with on
the Northside of St. Louis, years ago - who taught
me so much, through laughter and tears. I never felt
alone or afraid, just felt alot of love. Chertil
Lumpkins, the words in this book are for
you. I remember the days hanging downtown,
trying to be cute, shopping at *Contempo* and going
skating, just real girly fun. God bless you and your
son.

And the words in this book are for Rita and
for others who had their babies young, in junior
high and high school and didn't know where their
futures would take them. The words in this
book are for my kids, my students at Scruggs
Accelerated Elementary School, The Wyman
Center and for my two little girls, Tamara and
Janelle Springfield, who I took to African dance
class and to the parks. I love you girls, I know your
life is blossoming. The words in this book are for
students and workers of color, who battle racism
everyday in schools and jobs. The words in this
book are for warriors like Rev. Al Sharpton, Queen
Afua and Dick Gregory.

The words in this book are for the burning
felt in my stomach, the tears I've cried, my growing
pains, my fears overcome and my "sunshine after
the rain." May your life be filled with unforgettable
journeys.

DuEwa Frazier
Brooklyn, NY
2002

Dedicated to my parents, both shining spirits
my mommy, Sylvia J. Wilson Frazier- a true warrior
and my daddy, Eric "Ngoma" Frazier - a future
jazz legend.

WHO AM I?

purple passionflower /ripe at any hour/ woman
gleaming/Black
woman/ strength streaming/womb dancing/I'm
dreaming/breathing/
dance that dance/ dance/I am dance/I am African and
woman and
daughter of God/ and createss/ and I rediscover my
ways/ I learn
from the music/ of my past dances/they are
wonderful and I speak
through my own music now/Thank you for the art
you gave
me/Thank you for my dancing life, Creator of All/ I
speak/I Am/I
speak/I Am
I AM ME
I AM

Foreword

Throughout time and history there have always been those people who through communal traditions and rites, step up to be the keepers of legacy, of honored traditions and spokespersons for their culture. Whether through song, dance, musical instrument, or word, the spoken word, keepers and spokespersons of culture, take responsibility to lend powerful and potentially world changing contributions, through their art. DuEwa Frazier - young poet, writer, teacher and performer, is one of these people. She is a spokeswoman for her culture.

In DuEwa's poetry you hear the stories of our great past, the times in which we ruled and reigned supreme. As this book's title suggests, most, if not all of her poetry, starts you on a journey, takes you somewhere, in your mind and speaks of the journeys of an African people, from past to present. Just as poetry is ancient, DuEwa, through her words, reminds us that , we too, are ancient and our ancient past is juxtaposed to our present. Reading *Shedding Light From My Journeys*, reveals that the royalty within us is accounted for and spoken for! Not only does DuEwa's poetry speak in lengthy tones regarding our history, it reflects the tenets of all the great griots. You can hear great poets like Nikki Giovanni, Sonia Sanchez and Gwendolyn Brooks in her poems such as "Journeys", "Us Creative Women" and "I Dream of Justice for Louima." These poems show love, freedom, beauty and a people's commitment to be bold, diverse, and understood.

These poems also urge us to embrace life's experiences as lessons of a journey and to live our lives like, "Yes, we once were Kings and Queens and we are that." From the actions and expressions which come from thinking, comes responsibility.

Likewise the pursuit of freedom through revolution also bears responsibility. DuEwa takes her writing seriously, takes her poetry seriously and through her words we realize we are great, we are free to be us, free to dream and free to journey. DuEwa has stepped up to the plate, now it is our turn.

Abiodun Oyewole
International poet, teacher and performer
Founding Member, The Last Poets
New York, NY
2002

TABLE OF CONTENTS

Journeys of Love

Son of My Sun

True, I cannot
believe it is you
who calms my
rivers with your
eyes, it is you
who calms my
nature with your
voice
My King from
soils so far away
that I have never
touched, but can
only imagine
Let me calm your
rivers with my quiet
storm
currents, ripples, and
waves flow within
to bring us into sync
How could it be
that I could be
so in tune to you
and you to me?
I look to the serene,
beautiful union that
will one day be yours
and mine
Son of my Sun
you are a twinkle
in God's eye, show
me the way ever
deeper into your
heart
My King,
touched with the
soul, genius
skill of body and

motion of a
thousand great
pasts,
As sure as the
sun meets
it's horizon
it is clear how
two paths
meet as
ONE

A Nu Love Space Demand

When you showed up
for me
that was proof
that love is a
reflection of me
you ask me how do
I want us to be?
I'll tell you
I want a love
that comes to me
speaking poetry
giving fruits
of love
like if I was hungry
on my last dollar
would you bring over
brown rice, beans
and collards
to cook for us?
serve us purified
water in
champagne glasses
and toast us
sitting cross legged
on hardwood floors?
A simple idea
but to me
love nonetheless
I ask because I
hope you would
and I want a love
where we create
space and time
to be together

cherish our differences
our similarities
and become quiet so
we can be together
and apart
and I want
a love who sees the
divine in me and
won't be afraid
to pray with me
a love
who can re-visit
my childhood places
see my ugliest faces
still accept me for
it all
and I want a love
I bring my best self to
a love that
honors woman and
man and child
as family
as a strong unit
and I envision a
love that's not
perfect, yet perfect
for me
and a love
that won't allow
me to go to sleep
angry
and a love who's
spirit shines so bright
his torch lights
my future
and I want a love

who's ready when
I am and we
won't have to
tug and pull at this
because this love
is blessed by God
and the space I prepare
for this love
is for two
hey love
can I have a word
with you?

On Dark Nights

On dark nights
while rain falls
amber incense
trails my bedroom
I lay beneath silk
sheets, bare and
sensitive to touch
Thoughts of your
touch flood my mind
I envision you
while you are away
as subtle transparent like
smoke wandering into
my bedroom window screen
You become full
with body and
prop me up in
your arms
kiss me with
sweet brown
honey kisses
Honey meets
amber
us face to face
you place
my hand in
yours
my lover man
cosmic man
my husband
cover me
with your
love from
my crown
to my toes

My spirit soars
I crave for
more of this
marriage between
two souls
One love
for me and you
so I will savor
what we do
on dark nights

Letter To Your Proposition

On our first meeting:
"Urrrhgn, urrrrrrhgn, urrrhgn
excuse me, you look so sweet
what is your name? I'd love
to take you out, to dinner sometime
can I call you?"
Many calls, days and months later,
I am taken by your charm and intelligence

To your proposition, I reply in this letter:
Your hugs take me in, make me
feel like crawling inside of you
where I can feel warm and cared for
Your eyes take me in, intently
desirously, in your eyes I see
all of the things you'd like to
share with me
In your eyes I see
your lusts fulfilled seven times
over
Oh to sip from my well of love
and soak yourself in my soul
uncommittedly
Your nose takes in the aroma of
me, my essence, what swells and
swirls around my be-ing

Be-ing me
be-ing in my wise self
my strong self
my vulnerable self
my seeking self
my creative self
my feminine self
my God self
These things you don't see
you don't understand that

I have a whole sea of beauty and
wonder within, would you take time
to get to know me? To delve into this
part of me?
Oh to sip from my well
of love and soak yourself in my soul
uncommittedly
If love is sharing
then what will you and I share
if you don't love me?
Not to make myself out to
be a victim, but perhaps I
look at this thang from a more
in depth disposition

Dinner, music and playing
pool are cool
but my friend
my gentleman caller
These things, be-lov-ed
are not enough for you to
sip from my well of love and
soak yourself in my soul
uncommittedly

For my heart is
what is most at stake
and if you don't intend to
play for keeps
don't bother to play
at all

Signed,
Knowing what I'm worth

Cities Away

I know you're
working hard
as you can
a son, a brother
a corporate man
you stated your
claim, you want
to be free
enjoy a bachelor's
fame like Puffy
but you never met
a flower like me
don't know the
joy a sacred love
can bring
how I came to
have this crush
is the poetic question
I sing

I won't lie, I haven't
planned to give up
what many men
may hope to swim in yes,
the treasure which
lies beneath my ...

no brother, that
is not how a
strong, true love
is made
I have affections
for you, it's true
love to hold you
and look into
your eyes
we are friends

not so called lovers
I know you have
so many female
others

Yet, if there comes
a day, when you
tire of the
games,
feeling
loves' blossom
just the same
as your heart
calls out my
name
and when dreams
of loving walks and
talks become the
reality that
you need,
then look me up
until then

I am cities
away
a single woman
with sacred heart
still your girl
friend

Journeys of Self

Butterfly

I found rainbows
in my eyes today
I found rainbows
in my mouth today
rainbows in my soul
and wings to fly, fly, fly
I saw myself weaving
in and out of my life
I saw myself
shedding old skin
a metamorphosis
of many colors
Liken me to a new soul
dancing into my new skin
I too am a wonder-filled creature
unfolding strange and free
Butterflies cannot be caught
You can't hinder a butterfly
just smile
bless it
and let-it-go
Release me
I, butterfly
unfolding
strange and
free

R Ju Iz Spanish

Mami, mami, ju
look so good, are ju
married ? I think in
a past life I was Spanish
cause the papis in the
hood, they talk to me
like I'm their sister, they
call me mami like
I am their
hermana cause I
look like one of them
now I know we all come
from the same African mold
different hair, different colorsnegro,
blanco, tan, rojo y amarillo

Af-ri-ca is where I'm from
watoto ya Africa
we are children of Africa
bidi bidi bidi bamba
bidi bidi bidi bamba
batita bati batita bati
when I dance to Salsa-Calypso
music I can't stop twisting and
stepping and moving my hips
and eyes like a coy Puerto Rican
princess and the 'rican brother
who's asked me to dance wants
to know my name and says,
'ay mami, jhwere ju from? you
dance like jure from home from
my home - mi casa es Dominica
Puerto Rico, Colombia, Cuba, Nu Yawk',

Nu Yawk Nu Yawk Nu Yawk baby
home, salsa, merengue, bamba
samba

26

home, home, home, home
Afro-Cuban-Carib drum beats
home, home, home, home
and I can't stop moving my hips
and eyes like a coy Puerto Rican
princess with fire at my feet because
I am sister to my Puerto Rican
brothers and sisters
la negra y africana mujer de la
espiritu

No Yella Girl

Ha ha ha ha
you jus a yella girl
a high yella girl
and you ain't cute
how Black is you?
how Black you gon'
be? Yo mama
white, is yo mama
white? She's so pale
she jus about white
These are the endless
tauntings from little
school girls who seemed
to live to drive a sister
often

I fought back
not with my fists
but with my my dignity
and holding my head up
high
not that I was better
but I screamed from the
inside
know me for me, for
my insides, not what I
look like
but no one heard
so I played the role,
often a confused one
as people
sometimes do

I hid myself often
wandering into the
depths of who I really
was

who I am
with my pen and my pad
but see only God really knew
the depths of me and who I
really was inside

See I was freer than
the plaid socks
around my ankles
and I was freer than the braids
with ribbons at the ends
that my mother put
in my hair

And I was freer
than those sad
notes I listened to
from Sade's
Is it a Crime

I, I could relate to
Sade's melancholy
words from her lovelorn
lips to the innocent peak
in my ears

I understood the notes of
this heart torn yella girl
so I journeyed
through many phases and
friendships asking, Is
this when I am free from other
people's perceptions of my
outward externity and even
perceptions of myself?

As a girl must grow up
I found ways to turn my
melancholy notes into

freedom songs
See I hummed that yella
away to John Coltrane's
Love Supreme
I danced that yella away
to the rhythm of djembe
drums

I loved that yella away
for the hearts of friends who
have crossed my path

I taught that yella
away to be a
guardian for children

And I wrote that yella
away in poems, letters,
stories, essays, tributes
and plays
to hear my voice
my own unique voice
and make a new picture
of me

I found what
prejudices we have
against one another for
complexion and color
just makes no sense
I am half of a dark-chocolate
man and half of a
vanilla-peach
woman
and yellow or brown or
tan or red
are within a brilliant
spectrum of who we are
For all you yella girls

out there who have
suffered bruised ego
for those who ask you
who are you and why
do you look the way
you do?
tell them

Like a butterfly I
represent a unique
and divine creation of
God, one of many colors
who cannot be labeled
or controlled and
bound by your limiting
perceptions and lack of
self love
With that
I am free to be
my beautiful,
Black me

Out of My Queen Self

You were a smooth, smooth
Afri-scent-trick brotha/smellin of
sweet oils/draped in the tommyz
or poloz/but on a good day/
a dashiki/You were looking
for a queen to com-pli-ment tha'
King in you/ if you hear what I'm
saying/a spiritual woman/who took
care of herself/made some money
looked real fly/You thought I was fly/
I was lookin for a king to com-pli-ment
tha Queen in me/an intellectual
who meditates on oc-ca-sion/ a brotha
with the gift of gab/who would woo-woo
me/with plenty kisses and such/a pseudo
Af-ri-can type/who could stand me doing
my own thing/whatever that was/you know
be able to handle me/a smooth smooth
sister/Smellin of sweet oils/draped in
modern clothing/but on a good day/a gele and
lapa/In between daze of love/coos and such/
I became too flashy for your cultural wayz/
too ed-u-ca-ted for your spiritual wayz/
too feminine for your male wayz/too organized
for your controlling wayz/too busy for

32

your la-zy wayz/too wes-tern for your
Af-ri-can wayz/and to think I pondered all of
this/please/truth be told/I don't live like an
African/I am African/til the day I die/I waz
changing every which way to please you/
questioning my very essence/and truest
intentions/how could I have a spiritual and
cultural love/with a brotha who can't
understand how I serve my own soul?/was
it ever worth it to/pray with you?/dream with
you?/meditate with you?/laugh with you/hold
hands with you?/study with you?/love you?
how can I share with you then be made to feel
guilty/about the strength and beauty upon
which I am sharing?/an unconscious love
awoke/when it looked like the verge/a tinge/
and a glimmer of misuse/no more stars/hearts
and laughter/once a free spirit/turned
disturbed/you came for my light then left/
when I had/ not a ray more/to give/cold
criticism I found was a
projection of the shortcoming you felt within/
I had to grow/through the joy/confusion/then
pain of it all/though you later realized
your errors/only to request me/to share/
my light/once more/I had to decline/cause

baby/I realized/the sun don't set/and don't
rise/on no one brotha/ 'less he is/The One/
I am every woman/and more/there is only
one me/God loves me as I am/and as I love
me/I see/I AM A QUEEN/waiting for my King/
to compliment me/as I grew/and opened my
eyes/I saw/that you/were not/are not/Him

Journeys of My Sisters

Us Creative Women

Oh I know I don't
fit your mold
the clarity in my voice
the stride in my step
my peculiar ways
well if you heard that
God broke the mold
when he made me:
Black women, African
women, Latino women,
us creative women
then you would know my
call is going out

Last call, last call
will all you creative women
please stand up?
You women who sing
from the depths of your
souls
you women painters and
sculptures molding us a
new world

You women who dream us
a colorful world and
become our:
writers, directors and producers
Did someone say producer?
"I produce. I produce babies ma'am"
Why yes, and you too mommy
Last call, last call
will all you creative women
please stand up

Calling all you women who
carry the swords of truth and courage

who carry the swords and legacies
of an ancestral past
"An ancestral past? Did someone
say an ancestral past? Teach my sister !"
You see we walk, carrying the strengths
and traditions of our foreparents
they stepped loudly
so that we may step softly and still
be heard, yes still be heard

Calling you women to shine, shine
round up men, women and children
to preach and teach about life,
love and survival

Calling you creative women
to stir up your souls and wear
the illustrious crowns of
griot woman
Queen mother
revered woman
legendary woman
Showing the world who
we are, who I am
you see
I lace the world with poetry
like Sonia Sanchez
I grace the world with song
like Mariam Makeba
I color the world with paint
like Lois Mailou Jones
I tell the story of a colored
girl like Zora Neale Hurston
I sprinkle the world with drama
like Rita Morena and Ruby Dee
and I dance, kick, twirl
like
Pearl Primus, Katherine Dunham,
Debbie Allen

passing down our stories
our songs, uninhibited and free
Let live the hands
let live the eyes
let live the voices
let live the minds
let live the feet
let live the ears
let live the SOULS
Band together
Calling all you creative women
I said band together all
you creative women
Calling all the Creator's
creative women to
rejuvenate and heal
us all

A Million Women

It was a million of
us that day, the
25th of October,
1997 in Philly town,
maybe even more
than a million
Each waking at
the crack of dawn
that day, some
even waking the
night before

A sacred call
was answered,
a call for us women
of all shades of brown,
regardless of our backgrounds
to meet, gather, convene,
rejoice, plan for ourselves,
our children, our communities,
our men

There were some babies
marching, and couples
without babies, and whole
families including a grandma,
uncle and cousin
some with canes,
and some in wheelchairs,
still they were with us

A million women
some tall, some short,
some dressed regal with
African cloth and eye catching
jewelry, others
in sweats and sneaks

All came to answer the call
to love ourselves more,
bond more with our men,
continue to be powerful
impacts on our children
and keepers of culture
wisdom and understanding
from our foreparents and
their traditions

Yes this march was also
for all of the women
who could not attend
There were some teachers
marching, some lawyers,
some students,
some factory workers,
some social workers,
some nurses, some
doctors, some natural
healers, writers, singers,
actresses and dancers
marching

All came to answer the call,
to hear such a powerful and
resilient women as Winnie
Mandela speak on our triumphs
and the long struggle for freedom
won

All came to answer the call
and become a part of history,
herstory in this case
but after all everything we
do touches our men folk,
it is all one history
It was a million of us that day
in Philly town, maybe more

and what a relief it was that
guards were down
And there were very few
frowns and
no one seemed to care
what this one had on or what
that one's hair looked like
cause it really was
about spirit
and I think they felt that
whether consciously
or unconsciously

And I too
was one in a
million women
seeking inspiration
seeking a message
seeking unity and
hey sister haven't
seen you in a while,
hope everything's
alright
And seeking laughter
and a part of myself
that lives in each one
of my million sisters
I answered the call
of a million women
because after all
we are all
one

Rebirth

Take me not for your
footstool because
my words are sometimes
soft
soft
soft

What happens to the little
girls
the little girls
the little girls
What happens to the little girls
who become women who give
too much
taught that it's love that will
set you free from insecurity
and fears that people call
unreasonable and physical pain
people say is only imagined

What happens to the little girls
who become women who give
too much
locating what you think is the heart
of a man behind the handsome face
with locks or the
Brooks Brother brotha
what you think is the heart of a
man passionate yet vulnerable
is really unavailable and unwilling
to be open the way you need

What happens to the little girls
who become women who give too much
too much love, too much time, too much loyalty,
too much admiration, too much adoration,
too much bending over backwardness

to soothe, cajole and change the
mind of an irrational, unavailable half-heart
you see prior strength turns to too little
self care
becoming weak, needy and unbalanced
in the eyes of your desire
What happens to the little girls
who become women who give too much
searching for self in the mold of another
left limp and dry, desperate with an
abundance of tears forming rivers
of your dreams around you
calling for rebirth, rebirth, rebirth

What happens to the little girls who
become women who give too much
God becomes your savior
a plea to guardians and Jesus
mental searches of your psychic past
and chaotic present come rushing to mind

Spiritual workings from the heavens
above wrap around your body and spirit
to come in and do your surgery
as you lay in the dark recovery of your soul
calling out for rebirth, rebirth, rebirth
You see, loss of self becomes
newfound identity
Love looks different now
the little girl smiles
the woman never forgets

for colored girls who consider therapy when insane moments are enuf

Insane moments like
the tears you cried
for a man
when you're love
wasn't sweeter than
the blackest berry
and you weren't
revolutionary enough
like Malcolm or Betty
though neither was he
still you wish you could
punch out his eyes
surprise!
now that's Black on
Black crime!
so where's divine love
you dreamed yourself
in now?

Insane moments like
sitting neatly and corporate
in front of your computer
at office 9 to 5
breathing in stale air
that couldn't be called oxygen
absorbing radiation
atomic bombs
wouldn't dwell in
and your backside itches
from pantyhose and
velcro like swivel
chair as you hustle
the mechanics of your
voice and strong hands
for duties which get you
paid bi-weekly

Serenity Now!
you want to scream
Seinfeld character style
aren't you worth
more than that?

Yet you dream of
entrepreneurial heights
and days when you'll
be a beautiful Black
man's wife
until then, you chase
C.R.E.A.M - cash rules everything
crushed American dreams
pray to God
yours come true

Now you know what's killing
you softly and only you can make the
change
Insane moments like giving
your every breath and ounce
of love to a man who
just isn't ready to be
your mate
to help you soar to
God's purpose for you
and his too
cause he only sees
his own path
yet you pay
with your body each
time you make love
and you know deep
down inside he's
only giving you
half of him
but you're already
married to his soul

was that really
your goal?

Insane moments
like days and nights you
long for someone to talk to
to urge you along your path
then you remember
all the men you know
want you in bed
that's why they listen
and all the sisters you
know are in relationships
or pursuit of some
they don't have time to
hear your plight of woman
power and can you say
cel-i-ba-cy ?

God makes everything
alright
Insane moments can have
you caught between what your
external life says and who you
really are

Insane moments are to be
learned from so you skip
some of the scars
and begin to love
live and heal your life
over and over again
now breath

Journeys of My Brothers

Listen to the Brothers (for my St. Louis brothers)

Listen to the brothers
shootin that verbal stuff
on the verge of summer
they catchin the breeze
the cool breeze with hints
of bar-b-que
honeysuckle
and near burnt out car engines
of '73 Monte Carlos
that roll down the alley way

Listen to the brothers
shout argue
pontificate claim
and disclaim
to the things they do
and did on this day
and yesterday
and days before
Saying things like
"Aw man" at the tops
of their lungs
and other words which
tell of lyin
sneakin
searchin
and hidin

Telling of another brother
they've been looking for
"Ah saw 'im, he was right
'round there on Hodiamont Ave."
Bottles clink like long stemmed wine glasses
giving toast on New Year's Eve
Those bottled spirits do fly
complimented by
laughter in the air

No care in the world
this is their time
A night of verbal frolicking
testifying, word exchanges in slight code
with undercurrents of
brotherly love and trust

It's all good , chilling on the stoops
getting lifted
all the while
the night air
and light of the moon
and light of street light
lamp posts
curl around their faces
and dance upon their
gestures

And they'll do the
same thing again
on the
next night

Nothin But Love for Red South (for Errol and all Southern men)

You say you're red
red-bone
red-herring
red-barron
do your dreads wear red?
or white as Carolina rice
or blue as ocean
hear rhythm of blues
base
smile comes cross
my midwest face
love rap
jazz
poetry, blues
and soul music
old as Africa gold
way back when
we were sold

Are you free?
Free to be a
reflection of me
but I'm not red
they call me yellow
title ain't mellow
it's from the south
talking with cotton
still in yo' mouth
iron Black man
cuss and greet with a
smile in the
same breath

You might be on the
golf course with
your straw hat

or the cat
working at the
post office who
loves rap
you are that homeboy
with the platinum
gold teeth
you speak with
a drawl
that
makes southern
women weak

Our roots are
more than a
movie and
deeper than
roads that trailed
underground
southern parks
no longer
grow a rose like Rosa,
but we remember
why we ride in the
front of a bus
Erykah reminds us
all to let our bags go
Jill Scott asks us to take
a long walk, real slow

lyrically speaking
herstory so you would
know
peace to my brothas in the south
and every which way
the wind blows

MCs - No More Video Hos

What would hip hop be
without it's video chics?
the girls that
swoon and groove
gyrating to pulsating beats
rhythms of base
brotha MCs can you survive
without showing our sisters
bare breasted in g-strings
barely showing their face?
breaking their queenly
form so that you can form
your playa pimp daddy image
please

My sisters can you
get up off your knees?
from simulating lap dances prostitute prances
as the blinged out rap crew throws money at you?

Yeah it's fantasy in video
but how many brothers strive to live this life
never taking a wife cause our hip hop
videos don't glamorize a family life
sex sells
sex sells
the way my Black foremothers and fathers
were sold they made bucks
out our men and Black women's
bodies satisfied their sexual cravings
this we know
that the sexuality of
our people
has always been
exploited
and televised

But do you have to do it too?

Little Black girls on playgrounds pop
their coochies while singing their
favorite rap
little Black boys fantasize about
being with a little Black girl
seen in the news that some even
take it without asking in school bathrooms
schoolboy turned rapist
cause his eyes feasted
on the latest rap impresarios'
appetite for humping his video ho

Our modern day griots
our princes
our Kings
can you turn my sisters
from being your video b-tches
to being illustrious Queens?

I know it takes convincing
when you're used to
the bare naked of skin
but think again
these are your sisters
your next of kin
Back in the day rap was just
as popular without all
the bare booty stuff
so playas please

Please bring our sisters off their knees
show you have some class
show a remnant of respect
elevate your art it's not too late to start

The Epic Journeys

Journeys

I woke up one morning
I realized I had been journeying
for a long, long time
Car journeys, plane journeys,
on foot journeys, bus journeys,
subway journeys, dream journeys,
love journeys, spiritual journeys,
mental journeys, back and forth
journeys

That when you ariiiiiiiiiive to a place
you may not be there too long only to
get something valuable that you
came there for
The value
Freedom maybe
Love maybe
Forgiveness maybe
Creation maybe
Healing maybe
Peace maybe
A new beginning maybe
Something valuable that you
came there for

Our ancestors journeyed from
Africa land to a new world
this journey called
the Middle Passage
A frightful journey
a forced journey
a tearful journey
a suppressed journey
a new beginning journey
A history changed forever
of a people's journey
That when you ariiiiiiiiiive

to a place you may not
be there too long
only to get something
valuable that you
came there for
Our foreparents also journeyed
from the South of America land
to the North and all parts
this journey called the
Great Migration

A seeking journey
a new beginning journey
a step out on faith journey
a leaving the old journey
And so many more journeys
through time, time, time
Someone said to me the other day,
"Why isn't it amazing what too much
journeying can do to the soul?"
and I replied, "Not so, not if
you were supposed to be
journeying all the time"
you see journeys
connect you to
people, places and events
they make you appreciate
Life journeys

Sojourner Truth journeyed
Harriet Tubman journeyed
Matthew Henson journeyed
Frederick Douglas journeyed
Malcolm X journeyed
Assata Shakur journeyed

And so many more journeys
And I, and I

have been journeying
from the Kingdom of Heaven
towards my birth
from my mother's womb
to the world and on
through the flooooooow of
my life
The value of my journeys
are priceless
What are your journeys?

Rivers

I've known rivers
ancient, dusty rivers
and my soul
has grown deep
like the rivers, the rivers,
the rivers, like the

I've known rivers, rivers
of souls taken out of my
sacred village home one day
rivers of gold and diamonds
taken out of my land one day
rivers of bodies shackled
shackled and tackeled
thrown into dark holes of
cells one day

Rivers of bodies piled on
ships, dank, dark and dusty
ships
Rivers of souls
rivers of souls traveling cross
rivers and oceans

I've known rivers of sweat
pouring off of every part of me
my body
my tired, broken body
sweat under mid-day sun and
the threat of a lash from the whip
of massas son
when I picked
when I picked
when I picked cotton
When I thought I'd shout
and let my soul oooze on out
of me

I've known rivers
rivers of my African and
Native American ancestors
moving cross land
trails of their tears falling
journeying with dry
mouths
hungry bellies
tired, tired bones
and bound souls

I've known rivers
of lynchings in darkness
and rivers of change
from civil right marches
but lynchings still happen
today in the
year 2000

And I've known rivers
of hoses on my back
dogs at my heels
wooden sticks
going crack around
my neck

I've known rivers of
stuff that tempts you
to lose your mind
rivers of crack cocaine
in my neighborhood
rivers of alcohol
flowing through
my veins
to numb the post
traumatic stress
I was born into
from slavery

that is

Rivers of escapism in my
life I have known
Rivers of racism
rivers of sexism
rivers of homeless
and hungry children
rivers of rape
rivers of murder
murder, murder
my soul cries
murder

Somebody catch them
for they've tried to
murder my soul
and they've stolen
my seeds
and run off with my
legacies
and stomped on my
creations

But I shall turn
it around
I will turn it around
for I know I am an
heir to rivers of greatness
and I am an heir to rivers
of love
And my people will
be blessed
cause we shall turn it
around
It takes rivers of us
to bring change to
the world
rivers of us raising

children
rivers of us making
change
rivers of love
rivers of love
rivers of God's love
rivers of our love
I say to you
I've known
riiiiiiiiiveeeeeeers

For more information
visit
www.duewaworld.com
www.twitter.com/duewa1

www.ingramcontent.com/pod-product-compliance
Lightning Source LLC
Chambersburg PA
CBHW031903170626
46807CB00004B/1865